U.S. Department of Justice

Office of Justice Programs

Office of Juvenile Justice and Delinquency Prevention

I0484024

Juvenile Offenders and Victims

National Report Series

Bulletin

Office of Justice Programs
Partnerships for Safer Communities
www.ojp.usdoj.gov

June 2004

This Bulletin is part of the Juvenile Offenders and Victims National Report Series. The National Report *offers a comprehensive statistical overview of the problems of juvenile crime, violence, and victimization and the response of the juvenile justice system. During each interim year, the Bulletins in the National Report Series provide access to the latest information on juvenile arrests, court cases, juveniles in custody, and other topics of interest. Each Bulletin in the series highlights selected topics at the forefront of juvenile justice policymaking, giving readers focused access to statistics on some of the most critical issues. Together, the* National Report *and this series provide a baseline of facts for juvenile justice professionals, policymakers, the media, and concerned citizens.*

Juveniles in Corrections

Melissa Sickmund

A Message From OJJDP

The biennial Census of Juveniles in Residential Placement provides the nation with a detailed picture of juveniles in custody—age, race, gender, offenses, adjudication status, and more. Conducted by the U.S. Bureau of the Census for the Office of Juvenile Justice and Delinquency Prevention, the census surveys both public and private juvenile residential placement facilities in every state.

This Bulletin presents the latest available national and state-level data from the census, portraying the 134,011 youth held in 2,939 facilities on October 27, 1999. Because the census does not survey adult facilities, the Bulletin draws on other sources for statistics on offenders younger than 18 who were held in jails and adult prisons. It also examines imposition of the death penalty for crimes committed by offenders when they were younger than 18.

Clear, comprehensive, reliable statistical information on juveniles in custody, such as that presented in this Bulletin, is an invaluable resource for policymakers and juvenile justice professionals. This information is essential not only for planning and operating juvenile residential facilities but also for understanding and preventing delinquency.

J. Robert Flores
OJJDP Administrator

The Census of Juveniles in Residential Placement profiles juvenile offenders in custody

Detailed data are available on juveniles in residential placement in the United States

Information on residents in juvenile custody is drawn from the Census of Juveniles in Residential Placement (CJRP). The U.S. Bureau of the Census administered the CJRP for the first time in 1997 for the Office of Juvenile Justice and Delinquency Prevention (OJJDP). The CJRP, which is conducted biennially, provides the nation with the most detailed picture of juveniles in custody that has ever been produced. It asks all juvenile residential facilities in the U.S. to describe each youth assigned a bed in the facility on the fourth Wednesday in October. The census does not include federal facilities or those exclusively for drug or mental health treatment or for abused/neglected youth.

The CJRP collects individual data on each juvenile offender in residential placement, including gender, date of birth, race, placement authority, most serious offense charged, court adjudication status, date of admission, and security status. Facilities also provide information about the housing of overflow detention populations, physical layout of the facility, separation of residents, counts of residents age 21 and older, and the use of locked doors and/or gates. These detailed data are collected on residents who meet all of the following inclusion criteria for the census:

■ Younger than 21.

■ Assigned a bed in a residential facility at the end of the day on the fourth Wednesday of October.

■ Charged with an offense or court adjudicated for an offense.

■ In residential placement because of that offense.

CJRP does not capture data on juveniles held in adult prisons or jails; therefore, in the CJRP data, juveniles placed in juvenile facilities by criminal courts represent an unknown proportion of juveniles incarcerated by criminal courts.

One-day count and admission data give different views of residential populations

The CJRP provides 1-day population counts of juveniles in residential placement facilities. Such 1-day counts provide a picture of the standing population in facilities. One-day counts are substantially different from annual admission and release data, which provide a measure of facility population flow.

Juveniles may be committed to a facility as part of a court-ordered disposition or they may be detained prior to adjudication or after adjudication while awaiting disposition or placement elsewhere. In addition, a small proportion of juveniles may be admitted voluntarily in lieu of adjudication as part of a diversion agreement. Because detention stays tend to be short compared with commitment placements, detained juveniles represent a much larger share of population flow data than of 1-day count data.

State variations in upper age of juvenile court jurisdiction influence custody rates

Although state custody rate statistics control for upper age of original juvenile court jurisdiction, comparisons made among states with different upper ages are problematic. While 16- and 17-year-olds constitute approximately 25% of the youth population ages 10–17, they account for nearly 50% of arrests of youth under age 18, nearly 40% of delinquency court cases, and more than 50% of juveniles in residential placement. If all other factors were equal, one would expect higher juvenile custody rates in states where older youth are under juvenile court jurisdiction.

In addition, differences in age limits of extended jurisdiction influence custody rates. Some states may keep a juvenile in custody for several years beyond the upper age of original juvenile court jurisdiction; others cannot. Variations in provisions for transferring juveniles to criminal court also have an impact on juvenile custody rates. If all other factors were equal, states with broad transfer provisions would be expected to have lower juvenile custody rates than other states.

Demographic variations should also be considered when making jurisdictional comparisons. The urbanicity and economics of an area are thought to be related to crime and custody rates. Available bedspace also influences custody rates, particularly in rural areas.

The 1999 profile of residents in juvenile custody facilities was similar to the 1997 profile

Nearly 8 in 10 residents were juveniles held for delinquency offenses

The vast majority of residents in juvenile residential placement facilities on October 27, 1999, were juvenile offenders (81%). Juvenile offenders held for delinquency offenses accounted for 78% of all residents. Delinquency offenses are behaviors that would be criminal law violations for adults. Status offenders accounted for a small proportion of all residents (4%). Status offenses are behaviors that are not law violations for adults, such as running away, truancy, and incorrigibility. Some residents were held in the facility but were not charged with or adjudicated for an offense (e.g., youth referred for abuse, neglect, emotional disturbance, or mental retardation, or those referred by their parents). Together, these other residents and youth age 21 or older accounted for 19% of all residents. These proportions changed little between 1997 and 1999.

Most serious offense	Youth in facilities on the census reference day			
	Number		Percent	
	1997	1999	1997	1999
All residents	125,805	134,011	100%	100%
Offenders	105,790	108,931	84	81
Delinquency	98,913	104,237	79	78
Person	35,357	38,005	28	28
Violent	26,498	27,221	21	20
Status	6,877	4,694	5	4
Incorrigibility	2,849	1,843	2	1
Runaway	1,497	1,083	1	1
Truancy	1,332	913	1	1
Other residents*	20,015	25,080	16	19

*Includes youth age 21 or older and those held in the facility but not charged with or adjudicated for an offense.

Note: The census reference dates were October 29, 1997, and October 27, 1999. For all tables in this Bulletin, detail may not add to totals because of rounding and totals may include categories not detailed.

Two out of three facilities are private, but they hold fewer than one in three juvenile offenders

Private facilities are operated by private nonprofit or for-profit corporations or organizations; those who work in these facilities are employees of the private corporation or organization. State or local government agencies operate public facilities; those who work in these facilities are state or local government employees. Private facilities tend to be smaller than public facilities. Thus, although there are more private than public facilities nationwide, public facilities hold the majority of juvenile offenders on any given day. In 1999, private facilities accounted for 61% of facilities holding juvenile offenders; however, they held just 29% of juvenile offenders in residential placement on the census reference day.

Facility operation	Number		Percent change
	1997	1999	1997–99
Facilities			
All facilities	2,844	2,939	3%
Public	1,108	1,136	3
Private	1,736	1,794	3
Tribal*	–	9	–
Juvenile offenders			
All facilities	105,790	108,931	3%
Public	76,335	77,158	1
Private	29,455	31,599	7
Tribal*	–	174	–

* CJRP did not include tribal facilities in 1997.

Between 1997 and 1999, the number of public facilities and the number of private facilities holding juvenile offenders each increased 3%. Overall, there was also a 3% increase between 1997 and 1999 in the number of juvenile offenders in

custody. Private facilities, however, experienced a disproportionate increase in their offender population (7%) compared with public facilities (1%).

Private facilities are an important custody resource

Private facilities hold a different population of offenders than do public facilities. Compared with public facilities, private facilities have a greater proportion of juveniles who have been committed to the facility by the court and a smaller proportion of juveniles who are detained (pending adjudication, disposition, or placement elsewhere).

Custody status profile, 1999:

Custody status	Facility operation			
	Total	Public	Private	Tribal
Total	100%	100%	100%	100%
Diversion	0	0	1	2
Detained	25	30	14	45
Committed	74	70	85	53

Facility operation profile, 1999:

Custody status	Facility operation			
	Total	Public	Private	Tribal
Total	100%	72%	27%	0%
Diversion	100	29	71	1
Detained	100	85	15	0
Committed	100	68	31	0

Public facilities held most detained (85%) and most committed juveniles (68%). Private facilities, however, held the majority of juveniles who were in residential placement as part of a diversion agreement in lieu of adjudication (71%). In addition, although status offenders were only 10% of offenders in private facilities, 65% of status offenders in residential placement were held in private facilities.

Juvenile facilities reported more juvenile delinquents in placement in 1999 than at any time since 1991

Juvenile facilities reported 51% more juvenile delinquents committed to residential placement in 1999 than in 1991

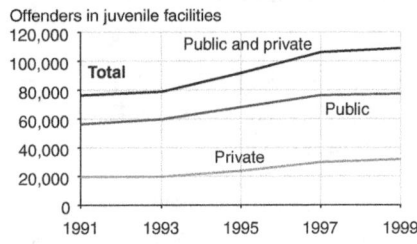

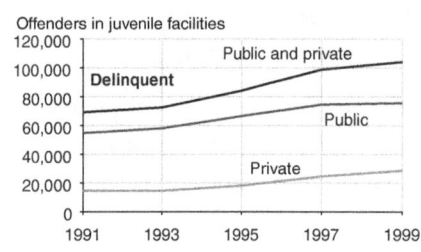

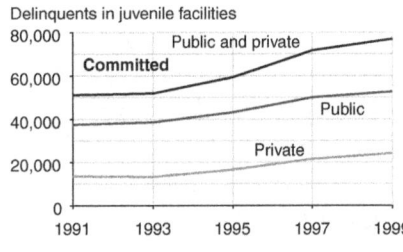

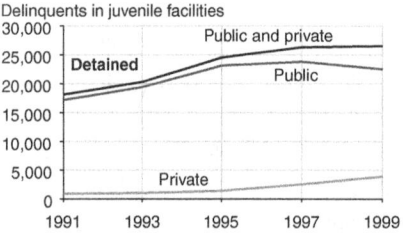

Custody status/ facility operation	Percent change in the number of residents				
	1991–93	1993–95	1995–97	1997–99	1991–99
Offenders					
Public and private	4%	16%	16%	3%	43%
Public	5	14	12	1	36
Private	−2	21	25	7	60
Delinquent offenders					
Public and private	4%	16%	18%	5%	50%
Public	6	14	13	1	38
Private	−1	24	37	17	98
Committed					
Public and private	2%	14%	20%	8%	51%
Public	3	12	16	5	41
Private	−1	23	31	13	79
Detained					
Public and private	12%	20%	7%	1%	46%
Public	13	19	3	−5	31
Private	6	44	79	61	340

Note: Juvenile offenders are youth under age 21 charged with a law violation (i.e., either a delinquency or a status offense). Committed juveniles are those in placement in the facility as part of a juvenile or criminal court-ordered disposition. Detained juveniles are those held prior to adjudication while awaiting an adjudication hearing in juvenile court, those held after adjudication while awaiting disposition or after disposition while awaiting placement elsewhere, and those awaiting transfer to adult criminal court or awaiting a hearing or trial in adult criminal court.

Source: Author's analysis of OJJDP's *Census of Juveniles in Residential Placement* [machine-readable data files] and *Children in Custody Census of Public and Private Juvenile Detention, Correctional, and Shelter Facilities* [machine-readable data files].

Is the increase in the custody population real?

Compared with data reported by public and private juvenile facilities in the 1991 Children in Custody census, the 1999 Census of Juveniles in Residential Placement data show a 43% increase in the number of juvenile offenders held and a 50% increase in the number of delinquents held. However, because the two data collections are not strictly comparable, it is impossible to determine if any of this apparent growth is actually an artifact of the change in methods. For example, the CJRP's October census date may have resulted in a larger count compared with the CIC's February date. In addition, the CJRP's roster format, more explicit definitions, and use of electronic reporting may have facilitated a more complete and accurate accounting of facility residents.

The data give support to the veracity of the trends since 1991

The data do, however, provide a strong indication that the changes are real. For example, it seems unlikely that the new CJRP method is merely counting more residents than the CIC method given that the population increases between the last wave of CIC data and the first wave of CJRP (i.e., between 1995 and 1997) were not necessarily the greatest biennial increases. In addition, the trends seen in the custody data are comparable to the trends observed in data from juvenile courts. Most telling is the fact that the CJRP data show an 8% drop in the number of status offenders held compared

Since 1995, the numbers of status offenders in custody have declined

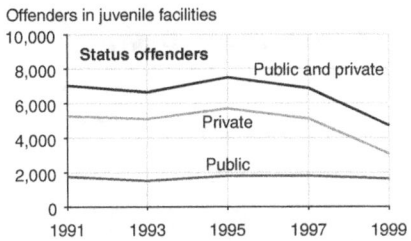

Offenders in juvenile facilities

Source: Author's analysis of OJJDP's *Census of Juveniles in Residential Placement* [machine-readable data files] and *Children in Custody Census of Public and Private Juvenile Detention, Correctional, and Shelter Facilities* [machine-readable data files].

with the last wave of CIC data. This provides even more evidence that the CJRP method is not merely counting more individuals than the CIC method.

For most status offense categories, fewer youth were in custody in 1999 than in 1997

From 1997 to 1999, the number of status offenders in both public and private facilities declined for all offense categories except underage drinking. The number of juveniles held in public facilities for underage drinking rose 68%, which more than offset the 12% decline in private facilities.

Percent change in the number of residents, 1997–99:

Most serious offense	Facility operation		
	Total	Public	Private
Status offense	−32%	−9%	−40%
Incorrigibility	−35	−10	−40
Runaway	−28	−2	−40
Truancy	−31	−25	−34
Underage drinking	18	68	−12
Curfew violation	−46	*	−57
Other status	−46	−25	−58

* Too few juveniles to calculate a reliable percentage.

Some declines were seen in the number of juveniles held for relatively serious offenses (such as homicide, robbery, and burglary)

Most serious offense	Percent change in the number of juveniles in residential placement, 1997–99		
	All facilities	Public facilities	Private facilities
Total juvenile offenders	3%	1%	7%
Delinquency	5	1	17
Person	7	2	24
Criminal homicide	−21	−25	40
Sexual assault	34	29	46
Robbery	−14	−11	−26
Aggravated assault	6	−3	54
Simple assault	12	8	18
Other person	50	40	82
Property	−1	−1	1
Burglary	−3	−4	1
Theft	−5	−8	2
Auto theft	−5	−5	−5
Arson	23	21	28
Other property	13	16	5
Drug	6	4	12
Drug trafficking	2	−3	18
Other drug	9	8	10
Public order	8	3	20
Weapons	−4	−5	−1
Other public order	17	10	31
Technical violation*	12	1	63
Violent Crime Index†	−3	−4	0
Property Crime Index‡	3	−2	21

■ In public facilities, the number of juveniles held for simple assault rose 8% and the number held for other person offenses not included in the Violent Crime Index rose 40%.

■ In private facilities, the number of juveniles held for simple assault rose 18% and the number held for other person offenses not included in the Violent Crime Index rose 82%.

■ There was a 12% increase in the number of juveniles held for technical probation, parole, or court order violations. The growth was driven by the change in private facilities (63%) rather than public facilities (1%).

* Technical violations = violations of probation, parole, and valid court order.

† Violent Crime Index = criminal homicide, sexual assault, robbery, and aggravated assault.

‡ Property Crime Index = burglary, theft, auto theft, and arson.

Source: Author's analysis of OJJDP's *Census of Juveniles in Residential Placement* [machine-readable data files].

The offense profiles were similar for those held in public facilities and those held in private facilities

Although public and private facility offense profiles were similar, public facilities had a greater proportion of juveniles held for Violent Crime Index offenses

| Most serious offense | Juvenile offenders in residential placement on October 27, 1999 | | | | | |
| | All facilities | | Public facilities | | Private facilities | |
	Number	Percent	Number	Percent	Number	Percent
Total juvenile offenders	108,931	100%	77,158	100%	31,599	100%
Delinquency	104,237	96	75,537	98	28,536	90
Person	38,005	35	28,056	36	9,897	31
Criminal homicide	1,514	1	1,368	2	141	<1
Sexual assault	7,511	7	5,154	7	2,352	7
Robbery	8,212	8	6,825	9	1,386	4
Aggravated assault	9,984	9	7,848	10	2,124	7
Simple assault	7,448	7	4,479	6	2,949	9
Other person	3,336	3	2,385	3	948	3
Property	31,817	29	22,725	29	9,051	29
Burglary	12,222	11	9,069	12	3,141	10
Theft	6,944	6	4,791	6	2,148	7
Auto theft	6,225	6	4,164	5	2,040	6
Arson	1,126	1	843	1	282	1
Other property	5,300	5	3,855	5	1,437	5
Drug	9,882	9	6,819	9	3,054	10
Drug trafficking	3,106	3	2,298	3	807	3
Other drug	6,776	6	4,521	6	2,247	7
Public order	10,487	10	7,380	10	3,087	10
Weapons	4,023	4	3,162	4	858	3
Other public order	6,464	6	4,215	5	2,229	7
Technical violation*	14,046	13	10,557	14	3,447	11
Violent Crime Index[†]	27,221	25	21,192	27	6,003	19
Property Crime Index[‡]	26,517	24	18,870	24	7,614	24
Status offense	4,694	4	1,623	2	3,063	10

- Compared with public facilities, private facilities held a smaller proportion of delinquent offenders and a larger proportion of status offenders.

- Juveniles held for aggravated assault made up 10% of offenders in public facilities and 7% of those in private facilities. Juveniles held for simple assault made up 6% of offenders in public facilities and 9% of those in private facilities.

* Technical violations = violations of probation, parole, and valid court order.

† Violent Crime Index = criminal homicide, sexual assault, robbery, and aggravated assault.

‡ Property Crime Index = burglary, theft, auto theft, and arson.

Source: Author's analysis of OJJDP's *Census of Juveniles in Residential Placement* [machine-readable data files].

Public and private facilities had different status offender profiles

Incorrigibility was the most common status offense category, especially for juveniles in private facilities. Private facilities held 77% of all incorrigibles in placement. Compared with private facilities, a larger proportion of youth in public facilities were held for running away or underage drinking.

Juvenile offenders in custody, 1999:

| Most serious offense | Facility operation | | |
	Total	Public	Private
Status offense	4,694	1,623	3,063
Incorrigibility	1,843	414	1,425
Runaway	1,083	477	606
Truancy	913	300	612
Underage drinking	378	189	183
Curfew violation	105	57	48
Other status	372	183	189

Status offense profile of residents, 1999:

| Most serious offense | Facility operation | | |
	Total	Public	Private
Status offense	100%	100%	100%
Incorrigibility	39	26	47
Runaway	23	29	20
Truancy	19	18	20
Underage drinking	8	12	6
Curfew violation	2	4	2
Other status	8	11	6

State custody rates in 1999 showed a broad range— from 96 to 632 per 100,000 juveniles

The U.S. custody rate did not change much from 1997 to 1999

In 1999, the overall custody rate in the United States was just 1% greater than the 1997 rate. However, there was substantial variation from state to state. In 20 states, rates declined or remained stable; rates increased in the rest of the country.

State of offense	Percent change in custody rate 1997–99
Rhode Island	–30%
Tennessee	–28
Maine	–25
Nevada	–18
Missouri, Montana	–17
North Dakota	–11
Hawaii, Washington	–8
Arizona, California	–6
Pennsylvania, Wisconsin	–5
Wyoming	–4
Alabama, Iowa, Nebraska	–3
Georgia	–1
Kansas, Maryland	0
Alaska, Connecticut	1
Louisiana, West Virginia	2
New Jersey, New York	3
Ohio, Oregon, South Carolina, Virginia	4
Dist. of Columbia, Indiana, Massachusetts, Mississippi	6
Colorado, Delaware	8
Florida, New Hampshire	9
New Mexico	11
Illinois, Kentucky, Minnesota, North Carolina, Texas	13
Michigan	14
South Dakota	16
Arkansas	18
Utah	31
Vermont	36
Oklahoma	40
Idaho	52

Nationwide in 1999, 371 offenders were held in juvenile facilities per 100,000 juveniles in the population

State of offense	Juvenile offenders in residential placement on October 27, 1999		State of offense	Juvenile offenders in residential placement on October 27, 1999	
	Number	Rate		Number	Rate
U.S. total	108,931	371	**Upper age 17 (continued)**		
Upper age 17			Oklahoma	1,123	273
Alabama	1,589	333	Oregon	1,549	404
Alaska	382	419	Pennsylvania	3,819	285
Arizona	1,901	334	Rhode Island	310	284
Arkansas	705	234	South Dakota	603	632
California	19,072	514	Tennessee	1,534	256
Colorado	1,979	407	Utah	985	320
Delaware	347	431	Vermont	67	96
Dist. of Columbia	259	704	Virginia	3,085	415
Florida	6,813	427	Washington	2,094	307
Hawaii	118	96	West Virginia	388	202
Idaho	360	220	Wyoming	310	488
Indiana	2,650	384	**Upper age 16**		
Iowa	1,017	296	Georgia	3,729	475
Kansas	1,254	383	Illinois	3,885	322
Kentucky	1,188	270	Louisiana	2,745	580
Maine	242	167	Massachusetts	1,188	206
Maryland	1,579	269	Michigan	4,324	417
Minnesota	1,760	290	Missouri	1,161	205
Mississippi	784	229	New Hampshire	216	167
Montana	246	220	South Carolina	1,650	441
Nebraska	720	342	Texas	7,954	370
Nevada	789	378	Wisconsin	1,924	338
New Jersey	2,386	273	**Upper age 15**		
New Mexico	855	378	Connecticut	1,466	513
North Dakota	235	297	New York	4,813	334
Ohio	4,531	345	North Carolina	1,429	221

Note: The rate is the number of juvenile offenders in residential placement per 100,000 juveniles age 10 through the upper age of original juvenile court jurisdiction in each state. U.S. total includes 2,645 juvenile offenders in private facilities for whom state of offense was not reported and 174 juvenile offenders in tribal facilities.

Source: Author's analysis of OJJDP's *Census of Juveniles in Residential Placement* [machine-readable data files].

Person offenders were 35% of juvenile offenders in custody nationwide; drug offenders were 9%

The offense profile for most states had a greater proportion of juveniles held for person crimes than for property crimes

State of offense	Most serious offense						State of offense	Most serious offense					
	Violent Index	Other person	Property	Drug	Public order	Status		Violent Index	Other person	Property	Drug	Public order	Status
U.S. total	25%	10%	29%	9%	23%	4%	Missouri	22%	7%	35%	7%	14%	16%
Alabama	9	13	27	7	32	11	Montana	20	12	41	5	20	2
Alaska	20	8	35	3	32	2	Nebraska	14	5	52	5	18	5
Arizona	9	14	32	17	26	3	Nevada	13	11	25	17	32	2
Arkansas	16	14	32	5	29	4	New Hampshire	15	40	25	1	11	7
California	34	7	28	7	23	1	New Jersey	24	5	20	22	21	9
Colorado	25	18	27	6	21	3	New Mexico	15	5	32	16	31	0
Connecticut	13	12	17	21	34	3	New York	32	7	26	11	10	14
Delaware	18	15	32	11	22	2	North Carolina	19	18	40	8	13	2
Dist. of Columbia	14	15	27	25	19	0	North Dakota	8	22	27	6	10	27
Florida	22	13	34	10	20	1	Ohio	27	8	31	8	22	4
Georgia	20	11	30	8	29	2	Oklahoma	33	6	37	6	13	5
Hawaii	23	13	36	3	23	3	Oregon	52	7	31	2	8	0
Idaho	21	15	28	3	31	3	Pennsylvania	18	13	20	12	31	5
Illinois	30	5	22	12	29	1	Rhode Island	29	11	21	17	20	1
Indiana	9	18	30	8	26	10	South Carolina	16	7	26	6	41	3
Iowa	16	19	35	8	17	5	South Dakota	11	10	33	5	35	6
Kansas	25	14	34	6	20	1	Tennessee	18	6	23	8	27	18
Kentucky	16	14	26	9	19	16	Texas	29	11	30	8	20	1
Louisiana	27	6	39	12	10	6	Utah	27	6	29	11	20	7
Maine	16	21	50	1	10	2	Vermont	27	18	31	0	9	13
Maryland	16	11	30	24	19	1	Virginia	21	11	26	7	30	4
Massachusetts	35	10	29	8	16	2	Washington	36	7	34	6	16	1
Michigan	27	9	30	5	18	12	West Virginia	19	10	29	8	20	14
Minnesota	21	12	28	5	26	8	Wisconsin	24	15	34	7	16	4
Mississippi	6	7	25	5	57	0	Wyoming	6	9	34	13	22	16

- Nationally, 29% of juveniles in residential placement were being held for property crimes. In comparison, 35% were held for person offenses (Violent Index plus other person offenses).

- States with the highest proportions of Violent Crime Index offenders were Oregon (52%), Washington (36%), Massachusetts (35%), California (34%), and Oklahoma (33%). North Dakota (8%), Mississippi (6%), and Wyoming (6%) had the lowest proportions.

- The proportion of juveniles held for drug offenses ranged from 25% in the District of Columbia to 1% in Maine and New Hampshire and 0% in Vermont.

Note: U.S. total includes 2,645 juvenile offenders in private facilities for whom state of offense was not reported and 174 juvenile offenders in tribal facilities.

Source: Author's analysis of OJJDP's *Census of Juveniles in Residential Placement 1999* [machine-readable data files].

Percent of juveniles held for Violent Crime Index offenses

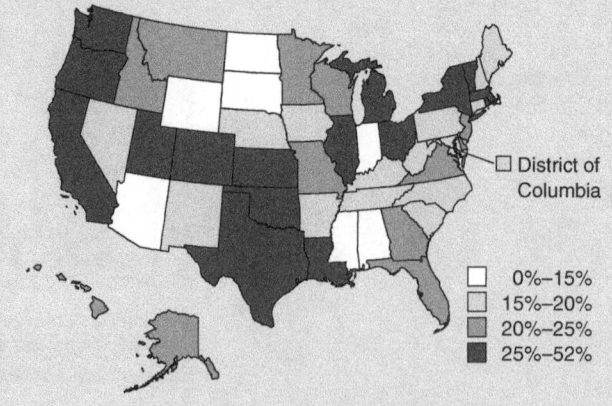

☐ District of Columbia

☐ 0%–15%
☐ 15%–20%
▨ 20%–25%
■ 25%–52%

Minority youth accounted for 7 in 10 juveniles held in custody for a violent offense in 1999

More than 6 in 10 juvenile offenders in residential placement were minority youth

On any given day in 1999, nearly two-thirds (65%) of juvenile offenders in placement in public facilities were minority youth. In private facilities the proportion of minority youth was just over half (55%).

Racial profile of juvenile offenders in residential placement, 1999:

Race/ethnicity	Facility operation		
	Total	Public	Private
Total	100%	100%	100%
White	38	35	45
Minority	62	65	55
Black	39	40	38
Hispanic	18	21	12
American Indian	2	2	2
Asian	2	2	2

Note: The census reference date was October 27, 1999.

The racial/ethnic profile in 1999 was similar to the profile of juveniles in custody in 1995. However, the 1999 data show a somewhat smaller proportion of minority youth in public facilities and a larger proportion in private facilities than the 1995 data.

Racial profile of juvenile offenders in residential placement, 1995:

Race/ethnicity	Facility operation		
	Total	Public	Private
Total	100%	100%	100%
White	37	32	53
Minority	63	68	47
Black	40	43	34
Hispanic	19	21	10
American Indian	2	1	2
Asian	2	3	1

Note: The census reference date was February 15, 1995.

Non-Hispanic black youth accounted for 55% of juveniles held for robbery and 65% of those held for drug trafficking

Racial/ethnic profile of juvenile offenders in residential placement, 1999

Most serious offense	Total	White	Black	Hispanic	American Indian	Asian
Total	100%	38%	39%	18%	2%	2%
Delinquency	100	37	40	19	2	2
Criminal homicide	100	23	44	24	3	6
Sexual assault	100	52	31	13	2	1
Robbery	100	19	55	22	1	3
Aggravated assault	100	29	40	25	2	3
Simple assault	100	43	37	15	2	1
Burglary	100	43	34	18	2	2
Theft	100	43	38	15	2	1
Auto theft	100	36	38	21	2	3
Drug trafficking	100	16	65	18	0	1
Other drug	100	30	47	20	1	1
Weapons	100	26	42	27	1	4
Technical violation*	100	39	39	18	2	2
Status	100	54	31	10	2	1

10% of non-Hispanic white youth in custody were held for a sexual assault, compared with 5% of Hispanic and non-Hispanic black youth

Offense profile of juvenile offenders in residential placement, 1999

Most serious offense	Total	White	Black	Hispanic	American Indian	Asian
Total	100%	100%	100%	100%	100%	100%
Delinquency	96	94	97	98	95	98
Criminal homicide	1	1	2	2	2	4
Sexual assault	7	10	5	5	7	3
Robbery	8	4	11	9	4	11
Aggravated assault	9	7	9	13	10	15
Simple assault	7	8	6	6	8	5
Burglary	11	13	10	11	13	12
Theft	6	7	6	5	6	5
Auto theft	6	5	6	6	7	8
Drug trafficking	3	1	5	3	1	1
Other drug	6	5	7	7	5	4
Weapons	4	3	4	5	2	7
Technical violation*	13	13	13	13	14	10
Status	4	6	3	2	5	2

*Technical violations = violations of probation, parole, and valid court order.

Note: Race proportions do not include youth of Hispanic ethnicity. Totals include a small number of youth for whom race/ethnicity was not reported or was reported as "other." Detail may not total 100% because of rounding or because all offenses are not presented.

Source: Author's analysis of OJJDP's *Census of Juveniles in Residential Placement* [machine-readable data files].

In nearly all states, a disproportionate number of minorities were in residential placement in 1999

In 1999, minority youth accounted for 34% of the U.S. juvenile population and 62% of juveniles in custody

| State of offense | Minority proportion | | | | | State of offense | Minority proportion | | | | |
	Juvenile population	Total CJRP	Detained	Committed Public	Private		Juvenile population	Total CJRP	Detained	Committed Public	Private
U.S. total	**34%**	**62%**	**62%**	**66%**	**55%**	Missouri	18%	41%	56%	37%	*
Alabama	35	59	63	60	55	Montana	13	41	*	37	*
Alaska	34	56	*	52	*	Nebraska	14	45	41	45	50
Arizona	43	60	58	63	52	Nevada	37	49	49	50	*
Arkansas	26	56	*	59	58	New Hampshire	4	13	*	22	*
California	59	79	72	84	70	New Jersey	37	84	81	87	60
Colorado	27	54	51	60	51	New Mexico	62	78	76	79	*
Connecticut	25	77	78	82	63	New York	41	70	81	76	58
Delaware	32	68	66	*	*	North Carolina	34	63	68	69	36
Dist. of Columbia	86	97	100	*	*	North Dakota	11	39	*	*	34
Florida	41	58	63	58	55	Ohio	17	47	51	46	42
Georgia	41	66	65	67	66	Oklahoma	26	48	42	54	44
Hawaii	75	91	*	*	*	Oregon	16	27	16	29	22
Idaho	12	19	*	22	*	Pennsylvania	17	64	57	71	66
Illinois	35	69	75	70	53	Rhode Island	18	55	*	68	38
Indiana	15	38	42	41	29	South Carolina	40	67	78	67	65
Iowa	7	25	23	27	26	South Dakota	16	42	*	43	*
Kansas	17	48	52	49	38	Tennessee	24	50	39	53	42
Kentucky	11	37	53	39	25	Texas	52	74	74	74	74
Louisiana	44	78	74	82	74	Utah	12	27	30	28	25
Maine	3	4	*	4	*	Vermont	3	*	*	*	*
Maryland	40	70	61	73	75	Virginia	32	63	63	63	67
Massachusetts	20	62	58	75	54	Washington	22	41	42	40	*
Michigan	23	55	54	47	60	West Virginia	5	22	18	*	25
Minnesota	12	45	52	46	41	Wisconsin	15	59	58	65	47
Mississippi	47	73	74	73	*	Wyoming	12	28	*	29	28

- Minorities accounted for 66% of juveniles committed to public facilities nationwide—a proportion nearly twice their proportion of the juvenile population (34%).

- In most states, minority proportions tended to be lower for youth committed to private rather than public facilities.

- In six states and the District of Columbia, the minority proportion of the total population of juvenile offenders in residential placement was greater than 75%.

*Too few juveniles in category to calculate a reliable percentage.

Note: The juvenile population is the number of juveniles age 10 through the upper age of original juvenile court jurisdiction in each state. U.S. total includes 2,645 juvenile offenders in private facilities for whom state of offense was not reported and 174 juvenile offenders in tribal facilities. Minorities include blacks, Hispanics, American Indians, Asians/Pacific Islanders, and those identified as "other race."

Source: Author's analysis of OJJDP's *Census of Juveniles in Residential Placement 1999* [machine-readable data files].

Minority proportion of juveniles in residential placement

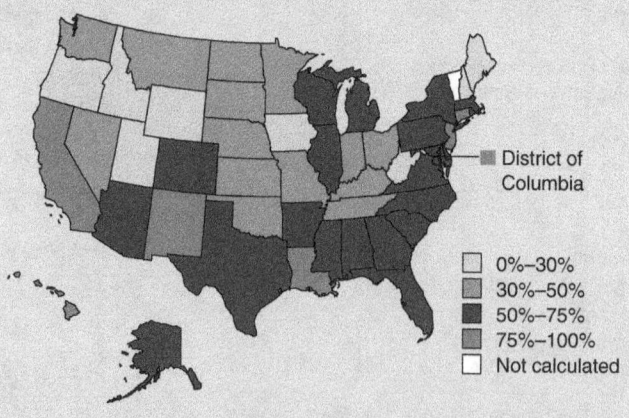

- District of Columbia
- 0%–30%
- 30%–50%
- 50%–75%
- 75%–100%
- Not calculated

Nationally, custody rates were highest for blacks

For every 100,000 non-Hispanic black juveniles living in the U.S., 1,004 were in a residential placement facility on October 27, 1999—the rate was 485 for Hispanics and 212 for non-Hispanic whites

State of offense	Custody rate (per 100,000)					State of offense	Custody rate (per 100,000)				
	White	Black	Hispanic	American Indian	Asian		White	Black	Hispanic	American Indian	Asian
U.S. total	212	1,004	485	632	182	Missouri	146	554	161	265	145
Alabama	208	588	249	314	93	Montana	148	1,463	614	652	704
Alaska	281	612	421	799	290	Nebraska	220	1,552	744	1,648	290
Arizona	234	957	473	293	125	Nevada	305	1,019	312	511	249
Arkansas	139	575	137	0	256	New Hampshire	150	1,278	578	0	0
California	269	1,666	623	612	238	New Jersey	70	1,108	327	0	6
Colorado	257	1,436	719	789	223	New Mexico	211	1,011	520	257	111
Connecticut	160	2,143	1,243	518	196	New York	169	1,119	143	466	34
Delaware	203	1,143	304	0	0	North Carolina	123	466	152	238	123
Dist. of Columbia	173	855	369	0	0	North Dakota	204	1,136	544	1,187	847
Florida	306	964	200	202	87	Ohio	221	1,038	430	112	75
Georgia	273	878	163	861	72	Oklahoma	194	821	297	343	56
Hawaii	39	87	90	0	121	Oregon	353	1,689	478	1,074	270
Idaho	203	871	344	278	173	Pennsylvania	123	1,230	902	154	249
Illinois	152	1,005	271	590	37	Rhode Island	155	1,363	680	0	474
Indiana	280	1,260	370	168	46	South Carolina	244	772	50	293	421
Iowa	240	1,726	545	1,231	465	South Dakota	436	2,908	1,091	1,653	1,235
Kansas	239	1,691	642	612	295	Tennessee	170	576	132	0	91
Kentucky	192	1,030	133	0	182	Texas	204	965	391	140	96
Louisiana	223	1,127	290	249	139	Utah	267	1,043	692	946	366
Maine	166	390	272	332	0	Vermont	93	698	0	0	0
Maryland	136	575	131	0	12	Virginia	225	1,024	323	166	104
Massachusetts	93	648	806	0	232	Washington	232	1,507	323	827	249
Michigan	243	1,058	1,112	428	215	West Virginia	166	1,060	251	0	292
Minnesota	183	1,504	630	1,783	459	Wisconsin	164	1,965	725	845	398
Mississippi	118	300	3,454	0	113	Wyoming	396	2,752	847	939	482

- In half of the states, the ratio of the minority custody rate to the nonminority white custody rate exceeded 3.3 to 1. In four states (Connecticut, New Jersey, Pennsylvania, and Wisconsin), the ratio of minority to nonminority rates exceeded 8 to 1.

- In Florida, Idaho, Maine, Nevada, Oregon, and Vermont, the ratio of minority to nonminority rates was less than 2 to 1.

Note: The custody rate is the number of juvenile offenders in residential placement on October 27, 1999, per 100,000 juveniles age 10 through the upper age of original juvenile court jurisdiction in each state. U.S. total includes 2,645 juvenile offenders in private facilities for whom state of offense was not reported and 174 juvenile offenders in tribal facilities. Minorities include blacks, Hispanics, American Indians, Asians/Pacific Islanders, and those identified as "other race."

Source: Author's analysis of OJJDP's *Census of Juveniles in Residential Placement 1999* [machine-readable data files].

Ratio of minority custody rate to nonminority white custody rate

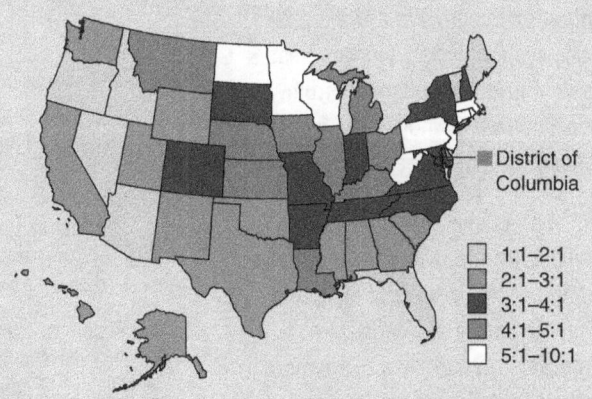

- District of Columbia
- 1:1–2:1
- 2:1–3:1
- 3:1–4:1
- 4:1–5:1
- 5:1–10:1

Minority disproportionality exists at various decision points in the juvenile justice system

Federal requirements on disproportionate minority confinement have changed

In 2002, the Juvenile Justice and Delinquency Prevention (JJDP) Act broadened the concept of disproportionate minority confinement to encompass disproportionate minority *contact* at all stages of the system. In 1999, when the data reported here were collected, the JJDP Act required that states determine whether the proportion of minorities in *confinement* exceeded their proportion in the population. States had to determine the extent of the problem and demonstrate efforts to reduce it where it exists.

Overrepresentation refers to a situation in which a larger proportion of a particular group is present at various stages within the juvenile justice system than would be expected based on their proportion in the general population.

Disparity means that the probability of receiving a particular outcome (for example, being detained vs. not being detained) differs for different groups. Disparity may in turn lead to overrepresentation.

Discrimination occurs if and when juvenile justice system decisionmakers treat one group of juveniles differently from another group based wholly or in part on their gender, race, and/or ethnicity.

Discrimination is one possible explanation for disparity and overrepresentation. This suggests that because of discrimination on the part of justice system decisionmakers, minority youth are more likely to be arrested by the police, referred to court intake, held in detention,

petitioned for formal processing, adjudicated delinquent, and confined in a secure juvenile facility. Thus, differential actions throughout the justice system may account for minority overrepresentation.

Disparity and overrepresentation, however, can result from factors other than discrimination. Factors relating to the nature and volume of crime committed by minority youth may explain disproportionate minority confinement. This suggests that if minority youth commit proportionately more crimes than white youth, are involved in more serious incidents, or have more extensive criminal

histories, they will be overrepresented in secure facilities even if no discrimination by system decisionmakers occurred. Thus, minority youth may be overrepresented within the juvenile justice system because of behavioral and legal factors.

In any given jurisdiction, one or more of these causes of disparity may be operating. Detailed data analysis is necessary to build a strong case for each causal scenario. However, on a national level, such analysis is not possible with the data that are available. For example, national data use broad offense categories such as robbery, which includes both felony and

---

Black juveniles are overrepresented at all stages of the juvenile justice system compared with their proportion in the population

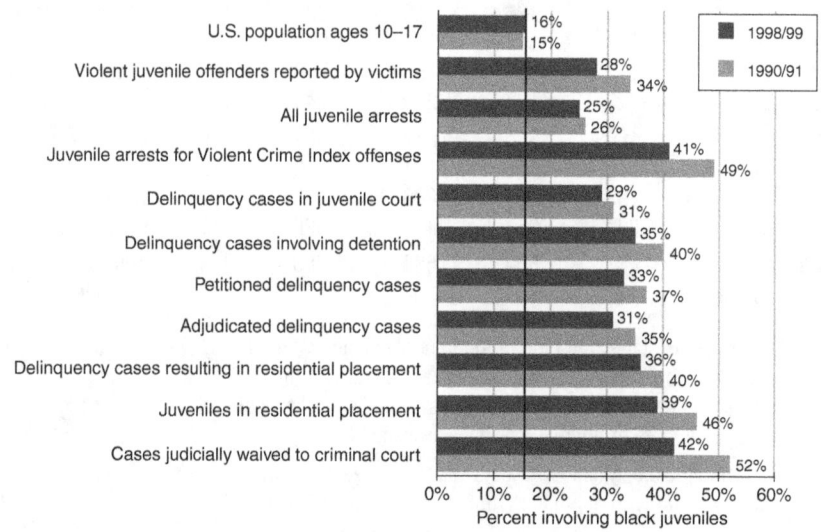

■ Nationally, for all stages of juvenile justice system processing, the black proportion was smaller in 1998/99 than in 1990/91.

Source: Author's analysis of U.S. Bureau of the Census' *Estimates of the Population of States by Age, Sex, Race, and Hispanic Origin: 1990–2000* [machine-readable data files] for 1991 and 1999; BJS' *National Crime Victimization Survey* [machine-readable data files] for 1991 and 1998; FBI's *Crime in the United States* for 1991 and 1999; OJJDP's *Juvenile Court Statistics* for 1991 and 1998; OJJDP's *Children in Custody Census of Public and Private Juvenile Detention, Correctional, and Shelter Facilities 1990/91* [machine-readable data files]; and OJJDP's *Census of Juveniles In Residential Placement 1999* [machine-readable data files].

nonfelony robberies. More severe outcomes would be expected for juveniles charged with felony robbery. Disparity in decisions regarding transfer to criminal court would result if one group of offenders had a higher proportion of felony robberies than another group (since transfer provisions are often limited to felony offenses).

The national data, however, do not support analysis that controls for offense at the felony/nonfelony level of detail. Similarly, although prior criminal record is the basis for many justice system decisions, criminal history data are not available nationally. Thus, at the national level, questions regarding the causes of observed disparity and overrepresentation remain unanswered.

NIBRS study reveals no direct evidence of racial bias in arrests of juveniles for violent crime

The Federal Bureau of Investigation's National Incident-Based Reporting System (NIBRS) data provide information on crime incidents reported to police, including characteristics of the crime, the victim, and anyone arrested for the crime, along with the victim's perception of the offender. An analysis of NIBRS data by Pope and Snyder looked for evidence of racial bias in the arrest of juveniles for violent crimes. Race was defined as white and nonwhite (including black, American Indian, Asian, and Pacific Islander). Both white and nonwhite racial categories included individuals of Hispanic ethnicity.

The study found that, for violent crimes, no difference in the overall likelihood of arrest of white juveniles and nonwhite juveniles existed after controlling for all other incident characteristics. The likelihood of juvenile arrest was affected, however, by several other incident characteristics independent of offender race. Arrest was more likely when there was a single offender, multiple victims, victim injury, or when the victim and offender were family members (rather than strangers). The odds of arrest also increased when the offender was male and when the victim was an adult or white. Because of the association of these other incident characteristics with offender race, a greater proportion of white juvenile offenders were arrested than were nonwhite juvenile offenders for most person offenses (e.g., robbery, aggravated assault, and simple assault).

For serious violent crime, data show that racial disproportionality begins with offending levels

Recent analyses of National Crime Victimization Survey data for 1980 through 1998 compared the rates of offending for black and white juveniles as reported by victims. The study focused on the serious violent crimes of aggravated assault, robbery, and rape because these are crimes in which victims have face-to-face contact with offenders.

Data from victims indicated that the serious violent offending rate for black juveniles is higher than the rate for white juveniles. For 1980–98, the offending rate for black juveniles was, on average, 4.1 times the offending rate for white juveniles. In comparison, the black-to-white ratio of arrest rates for these same serious offenses shows greater disparity than was found for offending. The average arrest rate for 1980–98 was 5.7 times higher for black juveniles than for white juveniles.

For both offending rates and arrest rates, though, the ratios of black to white rates have declined in recent years. From 1992 to 1998, the black-to-white rate ratios were very similar for arrests and

offending. On average, black juveniles had arrest rates that were 4.9 times greater and offending rates that were 4.6 times greater than the rates for white juveniles.

Because the analyses included only serious violent crimes, the findings cannot be generalized to nonviolent or less serious offenses for which law enforcement may have considerably more discretion in arrest decisions.

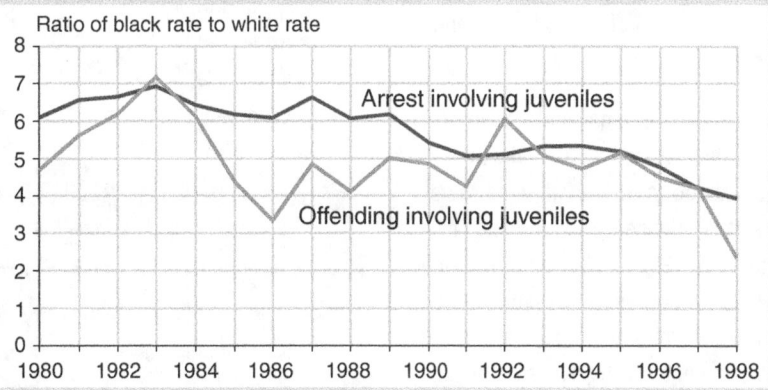

Source: Lynch's *Trends in Juvenile Violent Offending: An Analysis of Victim Survey Data.*

Females make up a small portion of the juveniles in custody, but require unique programming

Females accounted for 13% of juveniles in residential placement

The juvenile justice system is dominated by male offenders; this is especially true of the custody population. In 1999, males represented half of the juvenile population and were involved in approximately three-quarters of juvenile arrests and delinquency cases processed in juvenile court, but they represented 87% of juveniles in residential placement. The small proportion of female juveniles in residential placement was greater for private facilities (16%) than for public facilities (12%) and greater for detained juveniles (18%) than committed juveniles (12%). In comparison, the female proportion among those admitted to placement under a diversion agreement was large (40%).

More than one-third of females in residential placement were held in private facilities

Females in private facilities accounted for 35% of all females in residential placement in 1999. In comparison, private facilities held 28% of males in residential placement.

The proportion of females placed in private facilities varied substantially by offense category: 66% of all females held for a status offense were in private facilities, as were 42% held for simple assault, 25% held for aggravated assault, and 15% held for robbery. In general for both males and females, the less serious the offense category, the greater the likelihood the resident was in a private facility.

Females in residential placement tended to be younger than their male counterparts

Of all youth in custody, 30% of females were younger than 15 compared with 21% of males. For females in placement, the peak ages were 15 and 16, each accounting for approximately one-quarter of all females in placement facilities. For males, the peak ages were 16 and 17.

There was a greater proportion of offenders age 18 or older among males (14%) than among females (5%).

Age profile of residents, 1999:

Age	Total	Male	Female
Total	100%	100%	100%
12 and younger	4	4	5
13	6	6	9
14	12	11	17
15	19	19	24
16	24	24	24
17	22	23	17
18 and older	13	14	5

Females were more likely than males to be held for technical violations or status offenses

Offense profile for juvenile offenders in residential placement on October 27, 1999

Most serious offense	All facilities Male	All facilities Female	Public facilities Male	Public facilities Female	Private facilities Male	Private facilities Female
Total juvenile offenders	100%	100%	100%	100%	100%	100%
Delinquency	97	87	99	94	93	76
Person	36	30	37	32	32	27
Violent Crime Index*	27	15	29	18	21	9
Other person	9	15	8	14	11	17
Property	30	24	30	25	30	22
Property Crime Index†	25	20	25	20	25	19
Other property	5	4	5	4	5	3
Drug	10	6	9	6	10	7
Drug trafficking	3	1	3	1	3	1
Other drug	6	5	6	5	7	6
Public order	10	7	10	8	11	6
Technical violation‡	12	20	12	23	10	15
Status offense	3	13	1	6	7	24

■ Status offenders were 13% of females in custody in 1999, down from 23% in 1997. Person offenders were 30% of females in custody in 1999, up from 25% in 1997.

* Violent Crime Index = criminal homicide, sexual assault, robbery, and aggravated assault.

† Property Crime Index = burglary, theft, auto theft, and arson.

‡ Technical violations = violations of probation, parole, and valid court order.

Source: Author's analysis of OJJDP's *Census of Juveniles in Residential Placement* [machine-readable data files].

Minorities made up a smaller share of female than male residents

In 1999, minority youth made up the majority of males and females in residential placement. Non-Hispanic whites made up 47% of female and 36% of male juvenile offenders in residential placement. Among males, non-Hispanic black offenders represented the largest proportion (40%).

Racial profile of residents, 1999:

Race/ethnicity	Total	Male	Female
Total	100%	100%	100%
White	38	36	47
Minority	62	64	53
Black	39	40	35
Hispanic	18	19	13
Other	4	4	5

Note: Total includes a small number of juveniles for whom race was not reported.

Females accounted for a smaller proportion of minorities overall (11%) than of nonminority whites (17%) in residential placement in 1999.

Gender profile of residents, 1999:

Race/ethnicity	Total	Male	Female
Total	100%	87%	13%
White	100	83	17
Minority	100	89	11
Black	100	88	12
Hispanic	100	91	9
Other	100	84	16

Note: Total includes a small number of juveniles for whom race was not reported.

Nationally, the number of females in residential placement increased 2% from 1997 to 1999

State of offense	1999 female custody population	Percent change 1997–99 Female	Male	Female proportion 1999	State of offense	1999 female custody population	Percent change 1997–99 Female	Male	Female proportion 1999
U.S. Total	14,561	2%	3%	13%	Missouri	177	−22%	−16%	15%
Alabama	297	2	−7	19	Montana	30	*	−16	12
Alaska	60	*	14	16	Nebraska	180	−2	−3	25
Arizona	288	2	2	15	Nevada	147	−8	−8	19
Arkansas	132	*	5	19	New Hampshire	33	*	20	15
California	1,926	8	−5	10	New Jersey	189	7	6	8
Colorado	324	32	10	16	New Mexico	99	*	9	12
Connecticut	174	4	12	12	New York	921	−3	5	19
Delaware	45	*	4	13	North Carolina	162	−8	23	11
Dist. of Columbia	15	*	0	6	North Dakota	48	*	−15	20
Florida	960	50	10	14	Ohio	561	2	5	12
Georgia	582	−3	4	16	Oklahoma	150	19	43	13
Hawaii	27	*	−16	23	Oregon	192	−6	8	12
Idaho	51	*	45	14	Pennsylvania	411	−21	−1	11
Illinois	393	56	10	10	Rhode Island	21	*	−25	7
Indiana	615	24	2	23	South Carolina	243	7	4	15
Iowa	171	−25	1	17	South Dakota	90	*	18	15
Kansas	222	−20	7	18	Tennessee	282	−28	−27	18
Kentucky	231	26	7	19	Texas	768	10	16	10
Louisiana	327	−10	0	12	Utah	132	26	29	13
Maine	39	*	−27	16	Vermont	9	*	*	*
Maryland	156	16	4	10	Virginia	429	−13	11	14
Massachusetts	114	−21	17	10	Washington	261	−11	−5	12
Michigan	672	14	17	16	West Virginia	54	*	−5	14
Minnesota	306	19	15	17	Wisconsin	264	−19	−2	14
Mississippi	57	*	3	7	Wyoming	132	−4	−10	43

■ In nearly all states, females represented a relatively small proportion of the 1999 custody population—10% or less in 8 states and the District of Columbia.

* Too few juveniles in category to calculate a reliable percentage.

Note: U.S. total includes 2,645 juvenile offenders in private facilities for whom state of offense was not reported and 174 juvenile offenders in tribal facilities.

Source: Author's analysis of OJJDP's *Census of Juveniles in Residential Placement* [machine-readable data files].

Seven in ten juvenile offenders in custody were held in locked rather than staff-secure facilities

Security arrangements varied by facility characteristics

Juvenile residential placement facilities vary in their degree of security. The use of fences, walls, and surveillance equipment is increasingly common in juvenile facilities, although security hardware in juvenile facilities is generally not as elaborate as that found in adult jails and prisons. National accreditation standards for juvenile facilities express a preference for relying on staff, rather than on hardware, to provide security. The guiding principle is to house juvenile offenders in the "least restrictive placement alternative." Staff security measures include periodically taking counts of the youth held, using classification and separation procedures, and maintaining an adequate ratio of security staff to juveniles.

For each juvenile offender reported to the CJRP, respondents were asked if "locked doors and/or gates confined THIS young person within the facility and its grounds during the afterschool, day-time hours." Facilities reported that 7 in 10 juveniles were confined by at least one locked door or gate. The vast majority of juveniles in public facilities and in tribal facilities were confined under locked arrangements. For those in private facilities the reverse was true.

Facility security profile, 1999:

Type of facility	Total	Locked	Staff-secure
Total	100%	72%	28%
Public	100	87	13
Private	100	34	66
Tribal	100	91	9

As facility size increased, the proportion of juveniles held under staff-secure arrangements decreased. More than half (54%) of those held in facilities housing fewer than 40 residents were held under staff-secure arrangements, compared with 33% of those in facilities housing 40–109 residents and just 7% of those in facilities housing more than 270 residents. However, the majority of youth held in private facilities were housed under staff-secure arrangements, even in the largest facilities. In public facilities, though, 98% of those held in facilities with 270 or more residents were held under locked arrangements.

Facility security profile of residents, 1999:

Number of residents	Total	Locked	Staff-secure
All facilities	100%	72%	28%
Fewer than 40	100	46	54
40–109	100	67	33
110–269	100	79	21
270 or more	100	93	7
Public facilities	100	87	13
Fewer than 39	100	69	31
40–109	100	81	19
110–269	100	89	11
270 or more	100	98	2
Private facilities	100	34	66
Fewer than 39	100	27	73
40–109	100	40	60
110–269	100	34	66
270 or more	100	47	53

Security arrangements also varied by offense and placement status

A larger proportion of detained juveniles than committed juveniles was held in locked facilities.

Facility security profile of residents, 1999:

Type of placement	Total	Locked	Staff-secure
Committed	100%	66%	34%
Detained	100	88	12
Other	100	45	55

Juveniles in residential placement for homicide, robbery, and aggravated assault were the most likely to be held behind locked doors or gates.

Facility security profile of residents, 1999:

Most serious offense	Total	Locked	Staff-secure
Delinquency	100%	73%	27%
Person	100	76	24
Criminal homicide	100	90	10
Sexual assault	100	74	26
Robbery	100	82	18
Aggravated assault	100	79	21
Simple assault	100	63	37
Other person	100	74	26
Property	100	71	29
Burglary	100	74	26
Theft	100	68	32
Auto theft	100	69	31
Arson	100	76	24
Other property	100	69	31
Drug	100	70	30
Drug trafficking	100	77	23
Other drug	100	67	33
Public order	100	73	27
Weapons	100	77	23
Other public order	100	71	29
Technical violation	100	76	24
Status	100	29	71

Most status offenders were in staff-secure facilities in 1999

Unlike juveniles held for delinquency offenses, those in residential placement for status offenses were more likely to be confined under staff-secure than under locked arrangements. Seven in ten status offenders were confined under staff-secure arrangements. However, substantial variation existed within the status offense categories. Juveniles held for underage drinking or possession of alcohol were as likely to be held in locked arrangements as in staff-secure arrangements. Among those held for running away, curfew violations, and truancy, the

proportions of youth locked in were smaller. Juveniles held for incorrigibility were the least likely to be held under locked security arrangements.

Facility security profile of residents, 1999:

Most serious offense	Total	Locked	Staff-secure
All facilities			
Status offense	100%	29%	71%
Underage drinking	100	51	49
Runaway	100	40	60
Curfew violation	100	40	60
Truancy	100	24	76
Incorrigibility	100	18	82
Other status	100	33	67
Public facilities			
Status offense	100	55	45
Underage drinking	100	78	22
Runaway	100	60	40
Curfew violation	100	*	*
Truancy	100	47	53
Incorrigibility	100	43	58
Other status	100	59	41
Private facilities			
Status offense	100	14	86
Underage drinking	100	21	79
Runaway	100	23	77
Curfew violation	100	*	*
Truancy	100	13	87
Incorrigibility	100	11	89
Other status	100	8	92

* Too few juveniles to calculate a reliable percentage.

Security arrangements varied by demographic characteristics

Minority juveniles were more likely than nonminority juveniles to be confined behind locked doors. Among minorities, black and Hispanic youth were more likely to be held under locked arrangements than were other minorities.

Facility security profile of residents, 1999:

Race/ethnicity	Total	Locked	Staff-secure
White	100%	66%	34%
Minority	100	75	25
Black	100	75	25
Hispanic	100	76	24
Other	100	65	35

However, within more detailed offense categories, the difference between the proportion of white and minority youth held under locked arrangements diminished. This was especially true for those held for serious offenses. For example, among those held for robbery, 80% of white youth were confined by at least one locked door or gate compared with 83% of minority youth.

The proportion of juveniles held under locked arrangements increased with age. Although youth age 12 and younger were much less likely to be locked in than 17-year-olds, a substantial proportion of these youngest youth were locked in (63%).

Facility security profile of residents, 1999:

Age	Total	Locked	Staff-secure
12 and younger	100%	63%	37%
13	100	64	36
14	100	66	34
15	100	68	32
16	100	72	28
17	100	75	25
18 and older	100	81	19

Males were more likely than females to be held under locked arrangements.

Facility security profile of residents, 1999:

Gender	Total	Locked	Staff-secure
Male	100%	72%	28%
Female	100	65	35

Overall, much of the race/ethnicity, age, and gender differences in the proportion of juveniles held under locked rather than staff-secure arrangements were largely related to offense variations among the demographic groups.

On June 30, 2000, 7,600 youth younger than 18 were held in adult jails nationwide

Youth younger than 18 were 1% of jail inmates

According to the Bureau of Justice Statistics' Annual Survey of Jails, an estimated 7,600 youth younger than 18 were held in adult jails on June 30, 2000. These under-18 inmates accounted for 1.2% of the total jail population and have been less than 2% of the jail population since 1994.

Most jail inmates younger than 18 were convicted or awaiting trial as adult criminal offenders (80%). They were held as adults because they were transferred to criminal court or because they were in states where all 17-year-olds (or all 16- and 17-year-olds) are considered adults for purposes of criminal prosecution.

The number of youth younger than 18 in adult jails in 2000 was 19% lower than in 1999, but 14% higher than in 1994

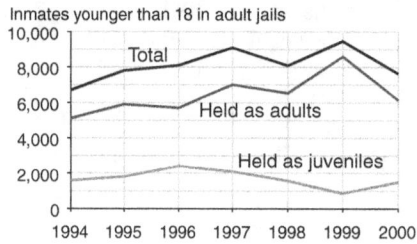

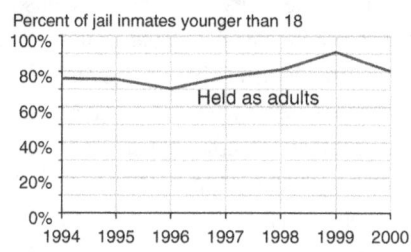

■ The number of jail inmates younger than 18 held as adults was 6,100 in 2000—down 29% from the peak of 9,500 in 1999, but up 20% from 1994.

■ The number of jail inmates younger than 18 held as juveniles rose 50% from 1994 to a peak of 2,400 in 1996, then dropped 38% between 1996 and 2000—a total decrease of 7% from 1994 to 2000. In comparison, the total jail inmate population (all ages) increased 28% between 1994 and 2000.

■ The vast majority of youth younger than 18 in adult jails in 2000 were convicted or awaiting trial as adult criminal offenders (80%). In 1999 the proportion reached 90%, but since 1994 it had not been below 70%.

Source: Author's adaptation of Beck's *Prison and Jail Inmates at Midyear 1999* and Beck and Karberg's *Prison and Jail Inmates at Midyear 2000*.

The Juvenile Justice and Delinquency Prevention Act limits the placement of juveniles in adult facilities

The Act states that "… juveniles alleged to be or found to be delinquent," as well as status offenders and nonoffenders "will not be detained or confined in any institution in which they have contact with adult inmates …." This provision of the Act is commonly referred to as the "sight and sound separation requirement." Subsequent regulations implementing the Act clarify this requirement and provide that brief and inadvertent contact in nonresidential areas is not a violation. The Act also states that "… no juvenile shall be detained or confined in any jail or lockup for adults …." This provision is known as the jail and lockup

removal requirement. Regulations exempt juveniles being tried as criminals for felonies or who have been convicted as criminal felons from the jail and lockup removal requirement. In institutions other than adult jails or lockups or in jails and lockups under temporary hold exceptions, confinement of juvenile offenders is permitted if juveniles and adult inmates cannot see each other and no conversation between them is possible. This reflects the sight and sound separation requirement.

Some temporary hold exceptions to jail and lockup removal exist: a 6-hour grace period that allows adult jails and lockups

to hold alleged delinquents in secure custody until other arrangements can be made (including 6 hours before and after court appearances) and a 48-hour exception, exclusive of weekends and holidays, for rural facilities that meet statutory conditions.

Some jurisdictions have established juvenile detention centers that are collocated with adult jails or lockups. A collocated juvenile facility must meet specific criteria to establish that it is a separate and distinct facility. The regulations allow time-phased use of program areas in collocated facilities.

Most youth sent to adult prisons are 17-year-olds, males, minorities, and person offenders

Youth younger than 18 accounted for 2% of new court commitments to state adult prisons

Thirty-seven states reported 1999 data to the National Corrections Reporting Program (NCRP). These states contain more than 87% of the U.S. population ages 10–17. Based on NCRP data from participating states, an estimated 5,600 new court commitments to state adult prison systems nationwide in 1999 involved youth younger than 18 at the time of admission. These admissions accounted for 2% of all new court commitments during the year. More than 3 in 4 of these youth were 17 years old at the time of admission. States with an upper age of original juvenile court jurisdiction below 17 made up half of all admissions of youth younger than 18.

Youth younger than 18 were 6% of all new court commitments to state prisons for robbery

In 1999, the proportion of new admissions involving youth younger than 18 was slightly higher for person offenses than for other types of offenses. The proportion of under-18 new admissions was 6% for robbery and 4% for homicide. In comparison, for most other offense categories the under-18 proportion of admissions was below 3%.

For youth younger than 18, the number of new admissions to state prison was nearly 65% greater in 1999 than in 1985

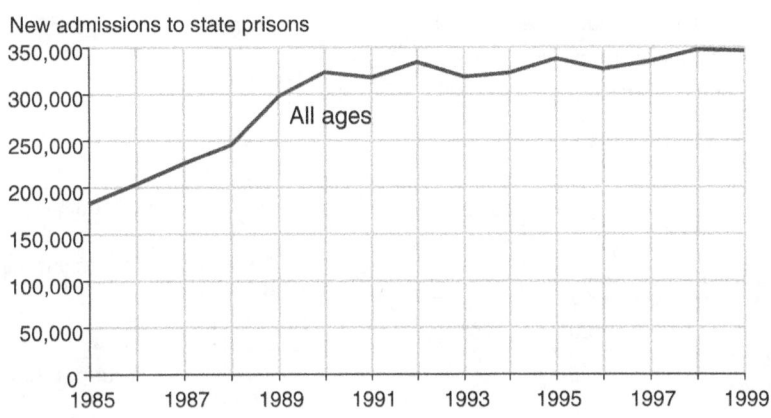

New admissions to state prisons

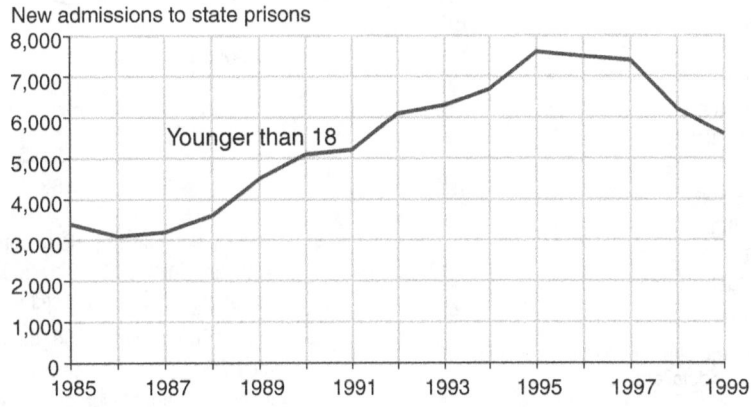

New admissions to state prisons

- On average, new admissions for youth younger than 18 rose 5% per year between 1985 and 1999. However, new admissions of those in this age group peaked in 1995 and dropped 26% by 1999.

- In comparison, the total number of inmates newly admitted to state prisons rose sharply from 1985 through 1990 (76%) and then leveled off.

Source: Author's adaptation of Strom's *Profile of State Prisoners Under Age 18, 1985–97*; Hughes and Beck's analyses of 1999 National Corrections Reporting Program data; and Beck and Karberg's *Prison and Jail Inmates at Midyear 2000*.

Of youth newly admitted to state prisons, 6 in 10 had committed a person offense

Compared with young adult inmates ages 18 through 24 at admission, new commitments involving youth younger than 18 had a substantially greater proportion of person offenses (primarily robbery and assault) and a smaller proportion of drug offenses (notably drug trafficking).

Offense profile of new admissions to state prison, 1999:

Most serious offense	Age at admission	
	Younger than 18	18–24
All offenses	100%	100%
Person offenses	62	36
Homicide	7	4
Sexual assault	5	4
Robbery	32	14
Assault	14	10
Property offenses	22	29
Burglary	13	15
Larceny-theft	3	5
Motor vehicle theft	3	3
Arson	1	1
Drug offenses	1	28
Trafficking	8	7
Possession	2	15
Public order offenses	5	7
Weapons	3	4

Note: General offense categories include offenses not detailed.

The vast majority of youth younger than 18 newly admitted to prison were male

Males accounted for 96% of new court commitments to prison involving youth younger than 18. Commitments of females younger than 18 primarily involved charges of robbery, assault, murder, burglary, and drugs.

The standing population of inmates younger than 18 held in state prisons in 2000 was 70% greater than in 1985

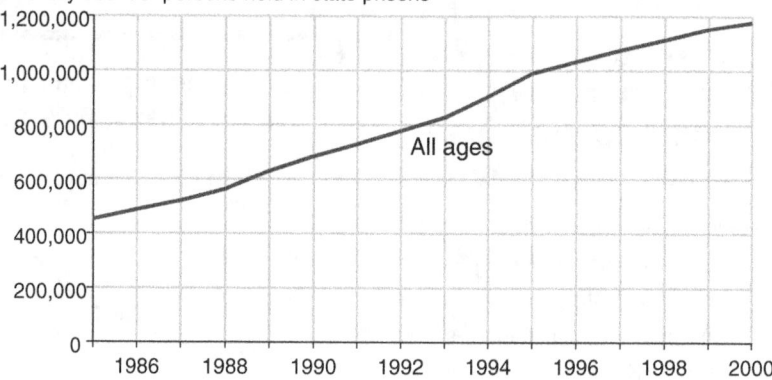

One-day count of persons held in state prisons

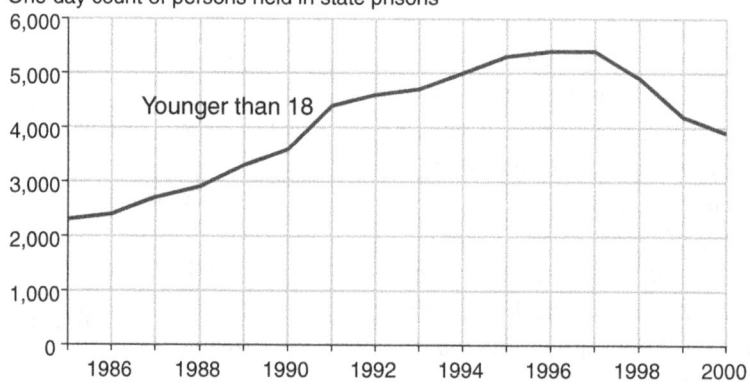

One-day count of persons held in state prisons

- The 1-day count of state prisoners younger than 18 grew 135% between 1985 and 1997 and then fell 28% by 2000, for an overall increase of 70%. In contrast, the overall prison population increased steadily from 1985 through 2000 (161%).

- From 1985 through 2000, the proportion of inmates younger than 18 remained less than 1%.

Source: Author's adaptation of Beck and Karberg's *Prison and Jail Inmates at Midyear 2000.*

Prisons differ from jails

- Jails are generally local correctional facilities used to incarcerate both persons detained pending adjudication and adjudicated/convicted offenders. The convicted population usually consists of misdemeanants sentenced to a year or less. Under certain circumstances, they may hold juveniles awaiting juvenile court hearings.

- Prisons are generally state or federal facilities used to incarcerate offenders convicted in criminal court. The convicted population usually consists of felons sentenced to more than a year.

Growth in under-18 prison admissions was greater for black males than for white males

From 1985 to 1999, prison admissions increased 38% for white males younger than 18 and 68% for black males in the same age group. Since 1995, however, the number of admissions in this age group has generally declined for both white and black males. During the period when the number of prison admissions for youth younger than 18 was on the rise, increases were greater for black males and recent declines have been greater for white males.

Robbery and aggravated assault accounted for a large proportion of the increase in prison admissions for both white and black males younger than 18. Unlike their white counterparts, however, black males also saw a large increase in drug admissions (from 30 to 490). In comparison, admissions of white males younger than 18 for drug offenses increased from 20 to 60.

Person offenses accounted for 66% of new admissions for young black males

Person offenses accounted for the majority of new admissions for both white and black males younger than 18. For whites, 56% of admissions were for person offenses—primarily robbery (22%) and aggravated assault (16%). For blacks, the proportion of admissions involving person offenses was higher (66%), stemming primarily from a greater proportion of robbery admissions (38%).

Blacks outnumbered whites nearly 2 to 1 among male under-18 prison admissions in 1999—the ratio was more than 8 to 1 for drug offenses

Most serious offense	New admissions to state prisons, under-18 males	
	White	Black
All offenses	1,800	3,200
Person offenses	1,000	2,100
Homicide	130	170
Sexual assault	80	110
Robbery	400	1,200
Aggravated assault	280	430
Property offenses	650	490
Burglary	390	290
Larceny-theft	110	60
Motor vehicle theft	60	70
Drug offenses	60	490
Public order offenses	70	140

- Black males accounted for 57% of all new admissions of youth younger than 18 to state prison in 1999.

- White males outnumbered black males among youth younger than 18 admitted for burglary and larceny-theft.

Note: General offense categories include offenses not detailed.

Source: Author's adaptation of Hughes and Beck's analyses of 1999 National Corrections Reporting Program data.

Among inmates released from state prison in 1998 who were younger than 18 when they were admitted, 78% were released before their 21st birthday

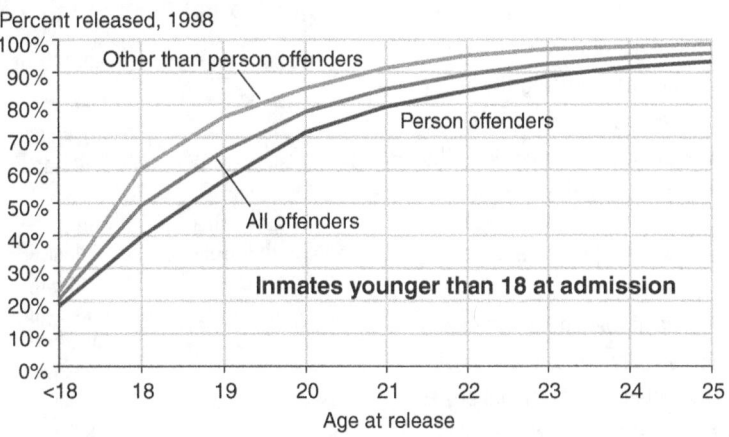

- Among inmates released from state prison in 1998 who were younger than 18 when they were admitted, 95% were released before their 25th birthday.

- A smaller proportion of person offenders younger than 18 were released from state prison before age 21 (72%) than was the case for other inmates younger than 18 incarcerated for offenses other than person offenses (85%).

- The average age at release among person offenders who were younger than 18 at admission was 20 years 6 months. The average age at release among those held for offenses other than person offenses who were younger than 18 at admission was 19 years 4 months.

- The average time served for inmates admitted before age 18 was just over 2 years 8 months. For person offenders, it was 3 years 4 months and for other offenders, it was about 2 years.

Source: Author's analysis of BJS' *National Corrections Reporting Program 1993–1998* [machine-readable data files].

Imposition of the death penalty for crimes committed at age 17 or younger remains rare

Supreme Court decisions prohibit the death penalty for youth younger than 16

The Supreme Court, in *Eddings* v. *Oklahoma* (1982), reversed the death sentence of a 16-year-old tried as an adult in criminal court. The Court held that a defendant's young age, as well as mental and emotional development, should be considered a mitigating factor of great weight in deciding whether to apply the death penalty. The Court noted that adolescents are less mature, less responsible, and less self-disciplined than adults and are also less able to consider the long-range implications of their actions. The Court, however, did not address the question of whether imposing the death sentence on the offender was prohibited because he was only 16 years old at the time the offense was committed.

In *Thompson* v. *Oklahoma* (1988), the issue before the Court was whether imposing the death penalty on an offender who was 15 years old at the time of the murder violated constitutional protections against cruel and unusual punishment. The Court concluded that the eighth amendment prohibited application of the death penalty to a person who was younger than 16 at the time of the crime. In *Stanford* v. *Kentucky* (1989), the Court stated that, "We discern neither a historical nor a modern societal consensus forbidding the imposition of capital punishment on any person who murders at 16 or 17 years of age. Accordingly, we conclude that such punishment does not offend the eighth amendment's prohibition against cruel and unusual punishment."

Youth younger than 18 are a small proportion of those receiving the death penalty

The Supreme Court decision in *Furman* v. *Georgia* (1972) struck down all existing death penalty statutes. Sentencing under post-*Furman* statutes began in 1973. The constitutionality of these current-era statutes was not determined by the Supreme Court until the 1976 decision in *Gregg* v. *Georgia*. Executions under the current-era statutes began in 1977. From 1973 through December 31, 2000, 200 death sentences have been handed down to 185 offenders who were younger than 18 at the time of their crimes. These death sentences account for less than 3% of the roughly 7,000 death sentences imposed on offenders of all ages since 1973.

As with most death sentences, death sentences for offenders younger than 18 are usually reversed. Since 1973, 95 offenders younger than 18 (51%) have had their death sentences reversed, 17 (9%) have been executed, and 73 (39%) remain under sentence of death.

Most death penalty states that specify a minimum age for the death penalty set the minimum at age 18

None specified	Age 16 or younger	Age 17	Age 18
Arizona	Alabama	Georgia	California
Idaho	Arkansas (14)[a]	New Hampshire	Colorado
Louisiana	Delaware	North Carolina[b]	Connecticut[c]
Montana[d]	Federal (military)	Texas	Federal (civilian)
Pennsylvania	Florida		Illinois
South Carolina	Indiana		Kansas
South Dakota[e]	Kentucky		Maryland
	Mississippi[f]		Nebraska
	Missouri		New Jersey
	Nevada		New Mexico
	Oklahoma		New York
	Utah (14)		Ohio
	Virginia (14)[g]		Oregon
	Wyoming		Tennessee
			Washington

[a] See Ark. Code Ann. 9–27–318(c)(2) (Supp. 1999).
[b] Age required is 17 unless the murderer was incarcerated for murder when a subsequent murder occurred; then the age may be 14.
[c] See Conn. Gen. Stat. 53a–46a(g)(1).
[d] Montana law specifies that offenders tried under the capital sexual assault statute be 18 or older. Age may be a mitigating factor for other capital crimes.
[e] Juveniles may be transferred to adult court; age can be a mitigating factor.
[f] The minimum age defined by statute is 13, but the effective age is 16 based on interpretation of U.S. Supreme Court decisions by the Mississippi Supreme Court.
[g] The minimum age for transfer to adult court by statute is 14, but the effective age is 16 based on interpretation of U.S. Supreme Court decisions by the state attorney general's office.

Note: Reporting by states reflects interpretations by offices of state attorneys general and may differ from previously reported age minimums. States not listed do not have the death penalty.

Source: Author's adaptation of Snell's *Capital Punishment 1999*.

At yearend 2000, 73 offenders were under sentence of death for under-18 crimes

Of the 73 offenders under sentence of death on December 31, 2000, for crimes committed at age 17 or younger, 55 were age 17 at the time of their offense and the remaining 18 were 16. Nearly half of these offenders (33 of 73) were not juveniles at the time of their offense—they were legally adults because they were older than their state's upper age of original juvenile court jurisdiction. The majority of these (26 of 33) were 17-year-olds from Texas, where original juvenile court jurisdiction ends at age 16.

The youngest of these 73 offenders was 19 years old as of December 31, 2000, the oldest was 42, and the average age was 25. As of yearend 2000, an average of 5½ years had passed since the offender's initial death sentence.

Most victims of these offenders were adults

More than 8 in 10 of the nearly 100 victims of these 73 offenders were adults. Of the victims whose demographic information was reported, most were non-Hispanic white (67%) and just over half (51%) were female. The majority of offenders were minorities (47 of 73); all were male.

Racial relationship between offender and victim, 2000:

Offender race/victim race	Percent of victims
Minority/nonminority	35%
Nonminority/nonminority	30
Minority/minority	30
Nonminority/minority	4

Note: Nonminority race are all whites who are not of Hispanic ethnicity; all others are minority.

Texas, Florida, and Alabama account for more than half of offenders sentenced to death from 1973 through 2000 for under-18 crimes

State	Offenders
Total	185
Texas	49
Florida	24
Alabama	20
Louisiana	11
Mississippi	11
Georgia	8
South Carolina	7
Arizona	6
North Carolina	6
Ohio	6
Oklahoma	6
Pennsylvania	6
Virginia	5
Missouri	4
Indiana	3
Kentucky	3
Nevada	3
Arkansas	2
Maryland	2
Nebraska	1
New Jersey	1
Washington	1

Source: Author's adaptation of Streib's *Death Sentences and Executions for Juvenile Crimes, January 1, 1973–December 31, 2000.*

1998 saw the first execution since 1973 of an offender who, under state statute, was a juvenile at the time of his crime; 1999 saw the first execution of an offender who was 16 at the time of his crime

Executions of under-18 offenders: 1973–2000

Name	Year of execution	State	Age at offense	Age at execution	Race/ ethnicity
Charles Rumbaugh	1985	TX	17	28	White
James Terry Roach	1986	SC	17	25	White
Jay Kelly Pinkerton	1986	TX	17	24	White
Dalton Prejean	1990	LA	17	30	Black
Johnny Frank Garrett	1992	TX	17	28	White
Curtis Paul Harris	1993	TX	17	31	Black
Frederick Lashley	1993	MO	17	29	Black
Ruben Montoya Cantu	1993	TX	17	26	Hispanic
Christopher Burger	1993	GA	17	33	White
Joseph John Cannon	1998	TX	17	38	White
Robert Anthony Carter	1998	TX	17	34	Black
Dwayne A. Wright	1998	VA	17	26	Black
Sean R. Sellers	1999	OK	16	29	White
Douglas Christopher Thomas	2000	VA	17	26	Black
Steve E. Roach	2000	VA	17	23	White
Glen Charles McGinnis	2000	TX	17	27	Black
Gary Graham (Shaka Sankofa)	2000	TX	17	36	Black

- All but 4 of the 17 offenders executed for crimes committed at age 17 or younger were from states where the upper age of juvenile court jurisdiction is 16 and were, therefore, legally adults at the time of their crimes.

- In 1998, Virginia executed a juvenile who had been transferred to criminal court under judicial waiver provisions. In 1999, Oklahoma executed a juvenile who was 16 at the time of his crime. Oklahoma statutes excluded 16- or 17-year-old offenders charged with murder from juvenile court.

- In 2000, four offenders were executed for crimes they committed at age 17.

Source: Author's adaptation of Streib's *Death Sentences and Executions for Juvenile Crimes, January 1, 1973–December 31, 2000.*

Sources

Beck, A. 2000. *Prison and Jail Inmates at Midyear 1999*. Bulletin. Washington, DC: Bureau of Justice Statistics.

Beck, A., and Karberg, J. 2001. *Prison and Jail Inmates at Midyear 2000*. Bulletin. Washington, DC: Bureau of Justice Statistics.

Bureau of Justice Statistics. 1999. *National Crime Victimization Survey* for the years 1991 and 1998 [machine-readable data files]. Washington, DC: Bureau of Justice Statistics.

Bureau of Justice Statistics. 2001. *National Corrections Reporting Program 1993–1998* [machine-readable data files]. U.S. Bureau of the Census (producer). Ann Arbor, MI: Inter-university Consortium for Political and Social Research (producer and distributor). Online: http://www.icpsr.umich.edu:8080/ICPSR-SDA/06823.xml.

Butts, J., Snyder, H., Finnegan, T., Aughenbaugh, A., Tierney, N., Sullivan, D., Poole, R., Sickmund, M., and Poe, E. 1994. *Juvenile Court Statistics 1991*. Washington, DC: Office of Juvenile Justice and Delinquency Prevention.

Federal Bureau of Investigation. 1992 and 1999. *Crime in the United States 1991* and *1999*. Washington, DC: U.S. Government Printing Office.

Greenfeld, L. 1989 and 1990. *Capital Punishment 1988* and *1989*. Bulletin. Washington, DC: Bureau of Justice Statistics.

Hughes, T., and Beck, A. 2002. Analyses of 1999 National Corrections Reporting Program data. Unpublished analysis. Washington, DC: Bureau of Justice Statistics.

Juvenile Justice and Delinquency Prevention (JJDP) Act of 1974 (Pub. L. 93–415, 42 U.S.C. 5601 *et seq.*) as amended (1992).

Lynch, J. 2002. *Trends in Juvenile Violent Offending: An Analysis of Victim Survey Data*. Bulletin. Washington, DC: Office of Juvenile Justice and Delinquency Prevention.

Office of Juvenile Justice and Delinquency Prevention. 1998 and 2001. *Census of Juveniles in Residential Placement 1997* and *1999* [machine-readable data files]. Washington, DC: U.S. Bureau of the Census (producer).

Office of Juvenile Justice and Delinquency Prevention. Various years. *Children in Custody Census of Public and Private Juvenile Detention, Correctional, and Shelter Facilities 1990/91, 1992/93,* and *1994/95* [machine-readable data files]. Washington, DC: U.S. Bureau of the Census (producer).

Office of Juvenile Justice and Delinquency Prevention. Formula Grants, Final Rule 61. *Federal Register* 65132, no. 238. (1996) (to be codified in 28 CFR Part 31).

Pope, C., and Feyerherm, W. 1990. Minority status and juvenile justice processing. *Criminal Justice Abstracts* 22(2):327–336 (Part I); 22(3):527–542 (Part II).

Pope, C., and Feyerherm, W. 1991. *Minorities and the Juvenile Justice System*. Research Summary. Washington, DC: Office of Juvenile Justice and Delinquency Prevention.

Pope, C., and Snyder, H. 2002. *Race as a Factor in Juvenile Arrests*. Bulletin. Washington, DC: Office of Juvenile Justice and Delinquency Prevention.

Puzzanchera. C., Stahl, A., Finnegan, T., Tierney, N., and Snyder, H. 2003. *Juvenile Court Statistics 1998*. Washington, DC: Office of Juvenile Justice and Delinquency Prevention.

Snell, T. 2000. *Capital Punishment 1999*. Bulletin. Washington, DC: Bureau of Justice Statistics.

Streib, V. 2001. *Death Sentences and Executions for Juvenile Crimes, January 1, 1973–December 31, 2000*. Juvenile Death Penalty Today. Ada, OH: Ohio Northern University.

Strom, K. 2000. *Profile of State Prisoners Under Age 18, 1985–97*. Special Report. Washington, DC: Bureau of Justice Statistics.

U.S. Bureau of the Census. 2001. *Estimates of the Population of States by Age, Sex, Race, and Hispanic Origin: 1990–2000* [machine-readable data files]. Washington, DC: U.S. Bureau of the Census.

This Bulletin was prepared under cooperative agreement numbers 95–JN–FX–K008 and 1999–JN–FX–K002 from the Office of Juvenile Justice and Delinquency Prevention, U.S. Department of Justice.

Points of view or opinions expressed in this document are those of the author and do not necessarily represent the official position or policies of OJJDP or the U.S. Department of Justice.

Acknowledgments

This Bulletin was written by Melissa Sickmund, Senior Research Associate at the National Center for Juvenile Justice, with funds provided by OJJDP to support the Juvenile Justice Statistics and Systems Development Program and the National Juvenile Justice Data Analysis Program.

The Office of Juvenile Justice and Delinquency Prevention is a component of the Office of Justice Programs, which also includes the Bureau of Justice Assistance, the Bureau of Justice Statistics, the National Institute of Justice, and the Office for Victims of Crime.

www.ingramcontent.com/pod-product-compliance
Lightning Source LLC
Chambersburg PA
CBHW080630180526
45168CB00007B/3110